3 Day Guide to Singapore

A 72-hour definitive guide on what to see, eat and enjoy in Singapore, Singapore

3 DAY CITY GUIDES

Copyright © 2015 BeautyBodyStyle, LLC

All rights reserved. No part of this book may be reproduced in any form or by any electronic or mechanical means including information storage and retrieval systems – except in the case of brief quotations in articles or reviews – without the permission in writing from its publisher.

Although the author and publisher have made every effort to ensure that the information in this book was correct at press time, the author and publisher do not assume and hereby disclaim any liability to any party for any loss, damage, or disruption caused by errors or omissions, whether such errors or omissions result from negligence, accident, or any other cause.

Image use under CC-BY License via Flickr

Cover Photo Credits:

Colorful Neil Rd. Photo by [Luke Ma](#)

Singapore. Photo by [Mac Qin](#) CC BY-ND 2.0

Sri Thendayuthapani Temple. Photo by [Allen Brewer](#)

Sri Veeramakaliamman Temple. Photo by [yeowatzup](#)

ISBN: 1507828993
ISBN-13: 978-1507828991

"The real voyage of discovery consists not in seeking new landscapes but in having new eyes."
– Marcel Proust

CONTENTS

1	Introduction	1
2	Singapore Day One	7
3	Singapore Day Two	18
4	Singapore Day Three	29
5	The Best Places to Party	38
6	The Best Places to Dine	42
7	Where to Enjoy a Good Night's Sleep	52
	Conclusion	61
	More from This Author	62

1 INTRODUCTION

Singapore. Photo by <u>Mac Qin</u> CC BY-ND 2.0

Singapore is a destination both pleasing and provoking to all of a travelers' senses. Imagine a breathtaking visual of the city's stunning panorama from Singapore's famed Altitude bar or a palatable lesson on how Chinese, Indian and Malay food cultures deliciously blend and interact in the local traditional cuisine. And let's not forget the riveting sounds of a visit to the Esplanade concert hall.

Singapore is not just a fully urbanized, bustling and

contemporary city that resulted from Singapore's rapid economic and industrial development. Singapore also has maintained its resplendent and arabesque nature values, as observed in the beautiful Bukit Batok Nature Park, as well as prodigious historical artifacts, temples and shrines that tell us arresting stories about the religion, traditions and customs of Singapore.

In a city where shopping destinations such as outlets, malls and districts exceed 100, be prepared to be exhausted with options. Whether you're a fashion lover or tech savvy guru you'll find the latest of what the world has to offer in the Musatafa Centre, Marina Square and Santec City to name a popular few.

History

Historically, the island was settled around 2nd century AD yet it was only in 1819 that the country we now know as Singapore was founded. Not long after, Singapore became the subject of fiery long-drawn disputes – first when its sovereignty was taken over by the British in 1824 and again during World War II, when Singapore was occupied by the Japanese. However it was in 1963 that Singapore gained its independence and became part of

Malaysia. Singapore was later proscribed from the group in 1965.

Soon after, Singapore experienced rapid development by boosting its education and industries, garnering fame by becoming one of the Four Asian Tigers – which in turn spurned the development of Singapore's tourism industry.

Climate and Seasons

It's worth pointing out that Singapore's temperature and weather does not change significantly throughout the year. The average temperature ranges from 22 to 35 °C (71- 95 °F) with the hottest months being April and May. While Singapore is a relatively warm city to visit, it is very humid with frequent rainfall so be sure to save space in your suitcase for a raincoat or umbrella at the very least. If milder temperatures are a must, plan your visit to Singapore between August and December, with the coolest temperatures being in the months of January and February.

Language

There are four official languages spoken in Singapore: Malay, Mandarin, English and Tamil. However among the inhabitants of Singapore the number of spoken languages exceed more than 20!

English is one of the main *lingua franca* to be used by traders and workers, therefore you shouldn't face too many challenges when communicating with the locals of Singapore, who are known to be quite hospitable and friendly.

Getting In

There are various modes of transport to reach Singapore with the most common being by airplane, landing at Chiangi Airport (http://www.changiairport.com/). Moreover, Chiangi Airport is known to be one of the most luxurious airports in the world, partly becoming a tourist attraction itself. This airport has become a crucial transition point in reaching Southeast Asia, therefore you will readily find several major airlines flying to Singapore. Chiangi Airport serves major airline carriers such as Air France, Finnair, Jet Airways and Turkish Airlines. If visiting Singapore is part of a larger trip in Southeast Asia, you may also consider taking one of the trains that connect the city with Kuala Lumpur and Malaysia. The trains run rather frequently and you can check the schedules and prices of international rail networks at http://www.ktmb.com.my/.

Changi Airport Singapore. Photo by Luke Ma

Getting Around

When it comes to traveling within Singapore, there are several options to navigate the city. Buses and trains are the most common mode of transport not only by foreign visitors but also for locals heading to jobs, schools and universities. Go for an S$8 city card which allows you to take any number of bus and train rides per day, granting you an easy commute from one side of the city to the other. Check out www.mytransport.sg/ for local schedules and information within Singapore.

Now, that you have a brief insight into the personality of Singapore, it is time to plan your 3 day adventure to experience Singapore from all its corners, be it physical or cultural. Let's begin with Day One.

2 SINGAPORE DAY ONE

Istana Green Foliage by <u>Terence Ong</u> *CC BY 2.5*

Prior to setting off on a day filled with cultural highlights, attractions and inspiring city gems, why not begin with a local breakfast to give you energy for the full day ahead. You'll start your exploration of Singapore at Istana Park, located in Central Area of Singapore, so it's best to have your breakfast nearby. Head to Orchard Road (approx. 10-minute walk from Istana Park) where you will find several cafes and hawkers working from the early hours of the morning. It is here that you will find Imperial Treasure Windows of Hong-Kong. This local eatery is open from 8am and serves Hong Kong Cantonese food, so expect to spot typical Hong Kong dishes such as congee (rice porridge) and rickshaw noodles on the menu. Prices are low with the average cost of a decent-size portion at S$9.

Imperial Treasure Windows of Hong Kong

Address: [#01-K1/24/25, TripleOne Somerset, 111 Somerset Road](#)

Opening hours: Daily from 8AM to 8.30PM

Phone: +65 67328798

Website: [http://imperialtreasure.com/en/restaurants/detail/tripleone/imperial-treasure-windows-of-hong-kong](#)

As mentioned earlier, this day will be a rather intense one, so it's best to have an early start– let's say at 9 or 10 AM as the latest. However if you are not an early bird, simply cross out a few points from the itinerary or, if possible, try to combine it with some other day of your trip. The distances covered during this day are short enough to be done by walking or cycling. There's not much need to take public transport (unless you really want to!).

The first point of interest on the tour of Day One is **Istana Park** – a place you hopefully had a glimpse of while enjoying breakfast. It is important to note that the chances of whether Istana Park and the residence will be open to the public for tours, strongly depends on the time of year you arrive. Istana Park is open to the public only few times per year (one of such occasions for example is Chinese New Year). A calendar of open days for 2015 can be found by visiting the following link: *http://www.istana.gov.sg/the-istana/open-house*

If you are lucky enough to arrive in Singapore on these special occasions, do not miss the opportunity to see the Istana Residency from inside. Not all the halls of the Presidential Residency are open to visitors but the tour gives fascinating insights into the architecture, history and functions of the gorgeous park surrounding this neo-Palladian style building. You will see several similar examples of

British military architecture around Singapore and other former British territories in Asia.

If the time of your visit does not match any of the opening days, you still have the opportunity to view the changing of the guards ceremony or take a peek at the park and residency from the main gate of Istana. Spend 1,5-2h here if the residency is open but if it is closed – not more than 30 minutes is needed to see the building and its park.

Istana Park, Orchard Road, Singapore 238823

2015 Residency Open House schedule:

http://www.istana.gov.sg/the-istana/open-house

2015 Changing of the Guards schedule:

http://www.istana.gov.sg/the-istana/ceremonial-guards

Opening hours: from 8.30am to 6pm;

Entrance fee: S$1 per person, guided tour inside the residency- S$2 per person

As you continue your day-tour, you should not miss visiting another beautiful park of Singapore – **Fort Canning Park.** You can get there by following the

Pennang Ln Street for 800 meters and passing Kith Café Park Mall. No matter which time of the day you visit the park, you will find locals and tourists alike enjoying a variety of activities – be it sightseeing, jogging, yoga or just walking along the nature trails.

Fort Canning Park is not only a place where notable festivals and concerts take place but it also has an important historical significance as it was home to 14th century Malay Palaces, later becoming the place where the Headquarters of Far East Command Center was situated. Moreover, at this exact location in 1942, it was decided that Singapore would surrender to the Japanese. Plan 1 to 2 hours to slowly learn about this park and its stunning mash-up of historical and nature heritage.

Park lighting hours: from 7AM to 7PM

More information on:

https://www.nparks.gov.sg/gardens-parks-and-nature/parks-and-nature-reserves/fort-canning-park

Sri Thendayuthapani Temple

Sri Thendayuthapani Temple. Photo by Allen Brewer

After leisurely strolling through the park, follow the River Valley to the west and then make a right turn on Tank Road for about 300 meters to view another remarkable site – **Sri Thendayuthapani Temple** (also known as Chettiar's Hindu Temple). This temple is the most sacred of all religious monuments of Singapore's Hindu community.

The astonishingly bright and architecturally impressive temple is known to be built in 1859 and through the ages it has successfully maintained its role and importance in Hindu practices. Each year the temple attracts thousands of Hindu pilgrims during the festival of Thaipusam.

Tourists are welcome to visit the temple however please ensure you respect the main principles of attending a Hindu temple: remove your shoes before entering, do not go to Sanctum part of the temple, dress modestly and maintain silence. Plan at least half-an-hour to be spent in the temple.

Sri Thendayuthapani Temple, 15 Tank Road, Singapore, 238065

Worshipping hours: from 8AM to 12AM noon, 5.30PM to 8.30PM

Phone: +65 - 6737 9393

Website: http://www.sttemple.com/index.asp

Orchard Road

The next point of interest will be Singapore's famed **Orchard Road** (located approximately 20 minute walk from Chettiar's Hindu Temple). Even if you do not consider yourself to be active shopper, this street can alter your attitude as every corner of this resplendent shopping district is designed to seduce each passer-by.

Orchard Road. Photo by chinnian

The street bustles with people, traders, colorful buildings and every kind of shop imaginable. Simply put? There is nothing you cannot find on Orchard Road. Be it the newest technology and gadgets, expensive fashion items or local souvenirs to be taken back home. As Singaporeans themselves call it, this urban oasis is the perfect spot for shopping and entertainment as you will find hundreds of stores, malls, shops, hotels, pubs, cafes and restaurants.

At the same time Orchard Road is also comprised of delightful green elements – trees, gardens and calming nature spots to relax and enjoy at a slower pace. If you would like to take your time exploring the many places along this boulevard, schedule to spend 1.5-2 hours.

Should you begin to feel the rumblings of afternoon hunger, dining options along the street include Asian food (Fat Cow restaurant, Imperial Treasure) as well as Western cuisine (Angus Steak house, California Pizza Kitchen and PS. Café among others).

Orchard Road, Singapore, Downtown Core

More information on:
http://www.orchardroad.org/information/

Singapore Botanic Gardens

After a full day of walking and sightseeing, its best to finish the day on a calm note. **Singapore Botanic Gardens** is situated around 5km from Orchard Road and to reach it faster, you can take buses number 7, 106 or 174 going every 15 minutes from Orchard Road. The vast and lush gardens are a true pleasure for those who enjoy the outdoors and being close to the nature.

One of the highlights of this surprisingly and

masterfully well-maintained area is **Orchid Garden.**

The garden includes an unbelievable number of over 60,000 beauteous plants and orchids adorning themselves in various shapes and vibrant colors.

Singapore Botanic Garden. Photo by edwin.11

Visitors are also welcome to visit the **Singapore Botanic Gardens Heritage Museum** to enrich their knowledge of the development and importance of maintaining these precious gardens. The gardens are rather spacious and it can take up to 3 hours for the dedicated visitor to walk through the entire area.

Singapore Botanic Gardens, Singapore 259569,

Singapore

Website: https://www.sbg.org.sg/

Opening hours:

Singapore Botanic Gardens: *Daily, 5am - 12am*

National Orchid Garden: *Daily, 8.30am - 7pm*

Jacob Ballas Children's Garden: *Tuesday to Sunday, 8am - 7pm (last admission: 6.30pm), closed every Monday*

SBG Heritage Museum: *Daily, 9am - 6pm. Closed every last Monday of the month*

3 SINGAPORE DAY TWO

Merlion Park. Photo by Gyver Chang CC BY-ND 2.0

With another adventurous day ahead, skip the typical and begin your next day with breakfast near the area of **Merlion Park**. As every local will tell you – hawker centers and small local street sellers are the best choice to satisfy early morning hunger.

For those who are not familiar with hawker centers, they are open-air complexes that incorporate a large number of stalls where hawkers sell inexpensive, cooked meals. If your hotel stay does not include free breakfast, hawker centers offer an affordable way for travelers to fuel up for the day ahead.

The optimum choice on your route will be Lau Pa Sat Festival Market (located around 2 kilometers from Merlion Park). Not only does this market successfully meet the needs of gourmands searching for diverse gastronomic experiences but it is also a visual point of interest with its distinctive design, shapes and elements that were created by British architect George Coleman. Expanding as a hawker center, Lau Pau has become a haunt for locals and foreigners alike providing them with an enormous selection of fast, cheap and delicious local meals.

Lau Pa Sat, 18 Raffles Quay, Singapore 048582

Working hours: Daily, 24 hours

Phone: +65 62202138

Website: http://www.laupasat.biz

Singapore is synonymous with the Merlion – a mythical character with the body of a fish and the head of a lion. The body of the fish reminds us that Singapore used to be a small fishing village and the lion's head reflects the etymology of city's name, as 'Singapura' in Malay translates to "the lion city".

The snow-white statue of this fish-lion creature was previously located at the mouth of Singapore River. However when the completed Esplanade Bridge obstructed the view of the statue from the bay, it was moved to Merlion Park where it can now be viewed along with the splendid scenery of **Marina Bay**.

Merlion Park, 1 Fullertone, Singapore

Asian Civilizations Museum

After a beautiful view of Merlion Park, it is time to visit one of the most intriguing museums in Singapore –the **Asian Civilizations Museum**. Taking into account the multi-faced cultural diversity of Singaporean society, a visit to this museum you will give you a broader insight into pan-Asian civilizations and their relationship with Singapore. The museum incorporates 11 vast galleries, each of them chronologically representing a specific period in Asian history, so at least 2 hours are recommended to peruse the complex.

Asian Civilisations Museum. Photo by hslo

To aid you in your discovery– the museum provides virtual hosts and interactive zones. Moreover, all the exhibitions are free of charge to its visitors and guided tours from volunteer guides are also available in various languages including English, French and Spanish.

Asian Civilizations Museum, 1 Empress Place, Singapore, 179555

Phone: +65 6332 7798

Website: https://www.acm.org.sg/home/home.html

Opening hours: Daily from 10am to 7pm, Fridays from 10am to 9pm.

Free of charge

Lunch-time hunger can readily be curbed at a remarkable restaurant within the Asian Civilizations Museum. The IndoChine Waterfront has gained a reputation for its authentic menu of Indochinese food and welcoming ambience. The restaurant provides fabulous river views and stands out not only for its quality of food but also for its philosophical and holistic approach in serving and preparing all meals.

IndoChine Waterfront, 1 Empress Place, Singapore, 179555

Phone: +65 6323 1043

Website: http://www.indochine-group.com/home/index.php

Working hours: From Sunday to Thursday from 12am to 3pm.

St. Andrew's Cathedral

St Andrew's Cathedral. Photo by <u>Bryn Pinzgauer</u>

After enjoying a delicious lunch, your next stop will be **St. Andrew's Cathedral** which is located only 600 meters from the museum (simply follow St. Andrew's Road as it is impossible to miss this high, bright white structure). Though it is smaller than most cathedrals found in Europe, St. Andrew's Cathedral majestically stands as the largest in

Singapore and serves as the mother church for dozens of congregations in Singapore. The church was built in the mid-19th century and represents the Neo-gothic architecture characteristic to many Anglican churches in Europe. The exterior of the cathedral is the most refined part of the church as its interior is rather modest. In contrast to the typical impressiveness of cathedrals, St. Andrew's Cathedral neatly represents the diverse aspects of religious and cultural influences in Singapore.

11 St Andrew's Road, Singapore 178959, Singapore

65 6337 6104

Website: http://www.livingstreams.org.sg/sac/

Bugis Street

Situated 2 kilometers away from the cathedral (this should not take you more than 30 minutes by foot) you can have a quick or not so quick (depending on how thick or thin your wallet became after yesterday's shopping activities) look at one of the most well-known and vast shopping streets in Singapore – **Bugis Street.**

In the fifties Bugis Street was a popular meeting and entertainment destination. It quickly garnered a reputation as the thoroughfare where transvestites rendezvoused, attracting the attention of sailors and other visitors to the city. Nowadays the street has been transformed into a diverse shopping district.

Bugis Street. Photo by <u>alex.ch</u>

Its modern environment now offers a large range of shopping, entertainment and relaxation services comprised of more than 800 stores and shops.

4 New Bugis St., Singapore 188868

Website: http://www.bugis-street.com/

Phone: (65) 6338 9513

Opening hours: Monday to Sunday 11AM – 10PM

Not far from Bugis Street and it's amazing shopping opportunities, you will a find a more informal shopping area that is perfect for interaction with locals. It's **Sungei Road Thieve's Market** – one of the most colorful and authentic street markets in Singapore. Locals go there to find useful, cheap items they need or to bargain for a better deal. Visitors can witness first-hand that the tradition of selling new and second-hand items – from old antique furniture and books to clothes and handicrafts – directly on the street has remained within the context of Singapore's urbanized environment.

Sungei Road Thieve's Market, Sungei Rd, Singapore 208785

Opening hours: Daily 11am - 7pm

Sri Veeramakaliamman Temple

Sri Veeramakaliamman Temple. Photo by yeowatzup

Near Sungey Road Flea Market one of the oldest temples in Singapore - **Sri Veeramakaliamman temple** – is situated. Even though it may seem like yet another Hindu temple to visit, it is well worth visiting as the temple's detailed, artistic and masterfully built exterior is visually impressive.

The temple was built by Tamil laborers, who named it in honor of the Hindu goddess Kali. The goddess is known as a protective force against evil, keeping the workers and worshipers safe in their new homes. Indeed, this temple has managed to escape the damage of war. As by some miraculous coincidence, the Japanese air raids during World War II did not hit (nor even scratch) the temple.

The Sri Veeramakaliamman temple is located in the district of **Little India,** known for its concentration of the Indian community and is also considered to be the most vibrant and culturally saturated parts of the city. The street food culture is very much alive in Little India and since it is almost dinner-time, you should definitely treat yourself to delicious Indian specialties like fish head curry which is renowned as a local delicacy favored by both locals and foreign visitors alike.

Sri Veeramakaliamman Temple, 141 Serangoon Road, Singapore 218042

Website: http://www.sriveeramakaliamman.com/

Operating hours: Daily, 5.30AM – 9.30PM

Little India MRT

60 Bukit Timah Road, Singapore 229900

Website: http://www.littleindia.com.sg/

4 SINGAPORE DAY THREE

Little India, Singapore. Photo by <u>yeowatzup</u>

The third day starts in the district where you ended Day Two – **Little India.** As this district is favored for its diverse gastronomic opportunities, it would be a shame not to start your morning in one of the local restaurants. If you have not decided where to have your morning meal, head for a café called MTR 1924. The specialty of the café is South-Indian food and it operates from the early morning hours, making it a great choice for breakfast.

MTR 1924, 438 Serangoon Road, Singapore, 218133

Phone: 6296 5800

Working hours: Mondays: Closed. Tuesdays to Sundays: 8.30am – 3:00pm, 5.30 pm – 10.00pm

Sri Srinivasa Perumal Temple

Sri Srinivasa Perumal Temple. Photo by Akuppa John Wigham

Hopefully, after breakfast at MTR 1924, you are ready to begin your final day exploring Singapore. **Sri Srinivasa Perumal Temple** has been chosen as the first object of interest. The temple which was constructed in 1855, is listed among the oldest Hindu temples in Singapore.

Like the Chettiar Hindu Temple, this temple also plays an important role for Hindu pilgrims during the Thaipusam Festival. Feel free to take pictures and enter the temple but bear in mind the requirements outlined in Chapter 1 explaining the **dos and don'ts** of visiting Hindu temples.

Sri Srinivasa Perumal Temple, 397 Serangoon Rd, Singapore 218123

Phone: 6298 5771

The Temple of Thousand Lights

The next stop will not be a Hindu or Christian sanctuary, but a Buddhist temple – **Sakya Muni Buddha Gaya Temple (The Temple of Thousand Lights).** Of all the Buddhist temples in Singapore, this is the most prominent and worth seeing – both as a place to observe Buddhsist rituals and a place to gain knowledge of the architecture of Buddhist temples, which in this case is characterized by the influence of Thai architectural slyles. As you cross the treshhold of the temple your eyes will immediatly rest upon the enormous statue of Buddha encircled by many, many lights thus explaining the second name of the temple (The Temple of Thousand Lights).

Sakya Muni Buddha Gaya Temple, 366 Race Course Rd Singapore 218636

Phone: (65) 6294 0714

Opening hours: Daily 8am - 4.45pm

Free admission

Burmese Buddhist Temple

As you walk around Little India, you will spot several more Buddhist temples along the way but there one other you should see for a key cultural reason. The **Burmese Buddhist Temple** is the only Burmese Buddhist temple in Singapore and also the oldest institution of Theravada. Theravada is a branch of Buddhist teaching based on Pali

Canon, whose instruction follows the ideas expressed in the **oldest** of Buddhist texts.

The temple was built in 1875 and it originaly stood on Kinda Road yet due to urban development, in 1988 the entire temple was moved to Tai Gin Road. Even though the temple is modest in size, due to its large concentration of statues and luxuriant details that will grab your attention, it is possible to easily spend 30-60 minutes here.

Burmese Buddhist Temple, 14 Tai Gin Road, Singapore 327873

Phone: (65) 6251-1717

Website: http://www.burmesebuddhisttemple.org.sg/index.htm

Bukit Brown Cemetery

Although you may have mixed feelings about going to cemeteries, it is worth taking a walk around **Bukit Brown Cemetery** as it will give you a new perspective on Singaporean culture and customs. Visiting graveyards and paying attention to the tombs and their characteristics can often tell a lot more than long lectures and books on local traditions.

Tombs at Bukit Brown. Photo by Jnzl's Public Domain Photos

The land of the cemetery used to belong to George Henry Brown – a businessman who arrived in Singapore in the mid -9th century. After his death it was bought several times – first from Ong Clan representatives using it for various purposes, such as housing and farming, and then by the local government, who was in need of territory to set up the Chinese Municipal Cemetery.

The cemetery is notable and popular not only among tourists but also culture and history enthusiasts as it reflects the values of Chinese culture and history in Singapore. Pay careful attention to the tombs and other details of the cemetery, as you appreciate the tranquil greenness which shapes the overall atmosphere of the cemetery.

Bukit Brown Cemetery, Lorong Halwa, Singapore

McRitchie Nature Trail

Now it is time for the final destination of your 72-hour tour -**McRitchie Nature Trail.** This trail is located 1,6km from Bukit Brown Cemetery and if you opt to walk, it should not take you more than 20 minutes to arrive. The trek along the trail will be the longest of your activities today (from 2 to 3 hours) so it's wise to eat beforehand. One option is to have a meal on the trail itself and if you fancy this idea, dine at Mushroom Café – a cozy locale offering simple and fresh meals to those who have finished or are just about to start the trail.

Mushroom Café, Thomson Road, McRitchie Reservoir

+65 6303 2358

Opening hours: Sunday-Saturday from 7AM to 9PM

*Website:
https://www.facebook.com/pages/Mushroom-Cafe/132013663503178*

MacRitchie Reservoir Park, Singapore. Photo by digitalpimp.

McRitchie nature trail is favored by sports and outdoors enthusiasts as it offers not only stunning and scenic views (the most amazing one is available from the Treetop Walk Bridge) but also various leisure activities such as canoeing and kayaking.

One of the main attractions of McRitchie Nature Trail is its 11 kilometer walking trail which goes around the oldest reservoir in Singapore, highlighted by forests and freshwater wildlife.

MacRitchie Reservoir Park, Singapore 298717

Website: https://www.nparks.gov.sg/gardens-parks-and-nature/parks-and-nature-reserves/macritchie-reservoir-park

Park Lighting Hours: 7:00pm to 7:00am

5 THE BEST PLACES TO PARTY

Clarke Quay, Singapore. Photo by <u>Luke Ma</u>

Singapore is known for its vivid atmosphere and the same characterizes the entertainment scene of the city, as even the pickiest of visitors will find a spot according to their taste.

In fact, it's not easy to provide a singular description of Singapore's nightlife as it is extremely variegated – from chic and glamorous night clubs for cocktail drinkers and techno music fans to alternative and underground clubs for those who like to explore the rich rock scene of Singapore.

ZIRCA

If you fancy huge crowds, a large selection of drinks and electro-music, head to ZIRCA Mega Club – a place where hundreds of party-lovers gather to dance, drink and socialize.

ZIRCA, Clarke Quay Block C The Cannery River Valley Road | #01-02 to 05 and #02-01 to 08, Singapore 179022

Butterfly Factory

If your taste leans less towards techno dictions and you are a huge fan of mainstream mishmash, Butterfly Factory is the right choice for you. What's great about Butterfly Factory is the fact that there are two separate rooms – one for hip-hop and r&b enthusiasts another – for crowds who like to dance on electro and indie music. Billed as one of the trendiest of Singaporean nightclubs, it's an ideal venue for groovin' the night away.

Butterfly Factory, 1 Fullerton, #02-02/03/04 Singapore 049213, Singapore

Phone: 65 6333 8243

Website: http://www.thebutterfactory.com/

Operating hours: Wednesday: from 11pm to 4am, Friday, Saturday & Eve of Public Holiday: from 11pm to 5am

Club Kyo

Another vibrant venue that cannot be skipped while exploring the party scene of Singapore, is Club Kyo – a Japanese bar designed based with a very minimalistic and contemporary approach. The end result is a unique ambience which you probably won't get elsewhere. It's the perfect spot to make new friends over refreshing Japanese beverages.

Club Kyo, 133 Cecil St, Singapore 069535

Phone: +65 8299 8735

Website: http://clubkyo.com/

Operating hours: Wednesdays and Thursdays from 6pm to 3am, Fridays from 6pm to 5am and Saturdays from 8pm to 5am.

Canvas

If energetic live music is what you seek, head to

Canvas. Canvas is more than just a nightclub; it functions as cultural platform for various artists and musicians. Canvas connects them with audiences who seeks art and content in their entertainment and leisure time. Canvas is also a great place to meet and interact with the creative scene of Singapore – photographers, musicians, film-makers, art-lovers, travelers etc.

Canvas, 20 Upper Circular Road, Singapore 058416

Phone: +65 6538 2928

Website: http://canvasvenue.sg/

Operating hours: Tuesdays from 3pm to midnight. Thursdays and Wednesdays from 3pm to 2am, Fridays from 3pm to 3am and Saturdays from 9pm to 4am.

No matter which part of the spectrum you fall into, one thing is clear – nightfall does not mean an end to Singaporean life. Instead, every night of the week its venues fill with revelers -be it blue-collar workers, tourists or chic socialites. So if you crave music and entertainment until daylight unpack your best shirt, don your favorite dress and hit the streets for unpredictable and exciting night out!

6 THE BEST PLACES TO DINE

Chicken wings BBQ, Singapore. Photo by Luke Ma

Singaporean culture incorporates a mixture of ethnicities such as Malay, Indonesian, Chinese and Indian, whose flavors have mingled and influenced one another. You will rarely see such a diversity of dishes as in Singapore, giving you countless local dishes to try, be it Bak Kut The (pork rib soup), Ban Mian (Chinese noodles served with vegetables, minced meat, egg and anchovy) or Hokkien Mee (rice vermicelli and yellow egg noodles that have been fried with cuttlefish, lard and shrimp).

The vast variety of spices, seafood, noodle types, sauces and preparation techniques forms the long list of local Singaporean cuisine. Nothing goes to waste when preparing food and even the brain and inner organs are turned into savory dishes, such as pig's organs soup. While it may be a slight culture shock to some, these are favored dishes within Singaporean cuisine so don't be surprised to find them on the menu.

As mentioned before, hawker stalls play a very important role in providing quick eats, making the Singaporean street food culture is incredibly strong and rich. Therefore a visit to Singapore without trying some of its incredible hawker food is simply incomplete. Nevertheless there are several world-class restaurants making Singapore a perfect destination for those who see travel as a way to engage in culinary explorations.

Cheap eats

Maxwell Food Center

Hawker centers are the cheapest of all the places where to eat as there it is easy to find meal in price categories from S$5 to S$10 and there are countless centers in Singapore.

Maxwell Food Center is one of the most popular of all the hawker spots in the city. It's comprised of stalls that treat the visitors to the best Tian Tian chicken rice and fish porridge in the area.

Maxwell Food Center, 1 Kadayanallur St, Singapore 069184, Singapore

Opening hours: Daily 8am - 10pm

Newton Circus

Newton Circus or Newton Food Center is another location where you will find a striking variety of hawker stalls selling both local and international dishes. As with rest of the hawker centers, the food costs next to nothing and it is possible to have a wonderful meal (try their famous chili crab or barbequed seafood) for just a few Singapore dollars.

500 Clemenceau Ave North Singapore 229495

Opening hours: Daily 12pm - 2am

Tiong Bahru Market

Every day of the week crowds of both tourists and

locals gather at Tiong Bahru Market to socialize and enjoy good food. The food here is very fresh and tasty, with the signature dish being the delicious roast duck or local specialty – chicken rice.

Tiong Bahru Food Centre, 30 Seng Poh Road, Singapore 168898, Singapore

Mid-range options

In Singapore, local cafes are a solid best option to dine at mid-range prices. There are hundreds in the city so chose accordingly to your desires – if you want something western, look for American cafes, if you want something Indian, check out the menu of any café you stumble upon while wandering around Little India. These cafes are also less crowded and you can enjoy your meal in a quieter ambience.

Standing Sushi Bar

Standing Sushi bar on Queen Street is well-known among local and foreign sushi fans and yes – you can (but it is not a must) eat while standing as it is done in original Japanese sushi bars. Average price per meal there is S$35 but if you happen to arrive during happy hour (after 5PM), you can get your meals even cheaper. If you do not know what to choose, try the salmon sushi and crabby chicken as these are among most favored of dishes offered.

Standing Sushi Bar, 8 Queen St, Singapore 188535

Phone:+65 6333 1335

Working hours: Mondays to Sundays 12:00 – 2:00 pm, 6:00 – 10:00 pm

W38Bistro and Bakery

If you would like to dine in a cozy atmosphere without the long wait, W38Bistro and Bakery is the place to go. The colorful and homelike café offers a stodgy breakfast on the weekends and has become particularly liked because of its extensive brunches and main dishes. A stack of fluffy pancakes will only set you back S$10 and for a huge Wagyu burger just S$20.

W38 Bistro and Bakery, 39 Jalan Mas Puteh, off West Coast Road, (S)128637

Opening hours: Tuesday - Friday: 11am - 10pm, Saturday, Sunday: 9am - 10:30pm. Closed on Mondays.

Bravery Cafe

Even though the name of cafe Bravery may lead you to believe entry requires guts and that only courageous ones are welcome to dine here, in reality Bravery Cafe is wonderful good-quality cafe that dishes up simple meals like smoked salmon sandwiches and other delights served with a variety of coffee and teas. S$20 is enough for you to eat like a king in the Bravery.

The Bravery, 66 Horne Road, Singapore 209073

Phone: 6225 4387

Opening Hours: Weekdays 9am - 7pm, weekends 8am - 8pm. Closed on Tuesdays (except public holidays)

Website: http://www.thebravery.com.sg

Deluxe Restaurants

Even though the plethora of dining opportunities provided by the expanse of hawker stalls and local cafes will meet you on every street corner, it nevertheless takes a bit more effort to find the best spot for those who are in a need of a five-star dining experience.

Singaporean cuisine scene thankfully does not

disfavor this segment and you will find many world-class restaurants that have raised the appreciation of even the most acrimonious food and restaurant critics.

Iggy's

For several years, Iggy's restaurant has earned its place among the best restaurants in Singapore, assigning it a prestigious status. The restaurant is located within the Hilton Hotel and in addition to its resplendent food selection, guests are treated to an extensive list of great wines.

The food at Iggy's is pricier (be ready to leave at least S$100 there) yet what you receive in exchange is not only an unforgettable experience but also a very unique approach in skillfully experimenting with various culinary traditions, esthetics and flavors.

The creativeness and gastronomic explorations of the chefs of Iggy's is something that astonishes many. Their signature dishes, many of which have remained on the menu for years like the capellini with sakura ebi, konbu and shellfish oil, are well worth a try.

Iggy's, 581 Orchard Road | The Hilton Hotel,

Singapore 238883, Singapore

Working hours: Sundays to Saturdays from 12pm to 2.30pm, 6pm to 10.30pm

Phone: 67322234

Website: http://www.iggys.com.sg

Les Amis

As prominent chefs from the world-over have opened their restaurants in Singapore, you will find plenty of restaurants representing other cuisines besides Asian ones. One such example is Les Amis restaurant whose menu consists of refined French cuisine.

Recommended dishes include the Lobster bisque with celeriac royale and seasonal black truffle. Or how about purple passion fruit in a hot soufflé served with a young coconut milk sorbet? The culinary French experience is presented in a luxurious environment, treating every visitor of the restaurant to an impeccable dining experience.

Les Amis, 1 Scotts Road, #01-16 Shaw Centre, Singapore 228208

Phone: (65) 6733-2225

Website: http://lesamis.com.sg

Working hours: Monday to Saturday. Lunch 12.00pm (Last seating at 2.00pm). Dinner 7.00pm (Last seating at 9.30pm). Closed on Sundays

L'Atelier de Joël Robuchon

L'Atelier de Joël Robuchon at Resorts World Sentosa is known for its innovative way of preparing and serving its quality meals. Visitors are given an observers view as the restaurant has removed the common barrier between the chef and the visitors.

Similar to many other prominent restaurants in Singapore, L'Atelier de Joël Robuchon exemplifies the concept of combining numerous culinary traditions. Here you will discover how the simplicity of Asian cuisine interacts with the refinement of French cooking techniques.

Foi grass burger and steak tartare is just one of the specialties of this remarkable restaurant which provides truly a delicious gourmand experience in every sense of the word.

L'Atelier de Joël Robuchon , 8 Sentosa Gateway, 101/103 Resorts World Sentosa, Hotel Michael

Level 1, Singapore 098269

Phone: +65 6577 6688

Website: http://www.rwsentosa.com/language/en-US/Homepage

Opening hours: Thursdays to Mondays: 6pm to 10pm

7 WHERE TO ENJOY A GOOD NIGHT'S SLEEP

Old Singapore. Photo by <u>Luke Ma</u>

While visiting Singapore, you may be overwhelmed by the amount of accommodation services that one can choose from. Indeed, as the number of tourists that arrive in Singapore continues to grow the accommodation industry refuses to sleep. Here are a few of the best suggestions from each price category in Singapore.

Budget-friendly accommodations

If your budget for the trip is modest, there are numerous cheap and comfortable places that are focus on accommodating budget travelers. Usually the accommodations in this category are hostels, where for the cheapest options one must share a room with other travelers. If this is not inconvenient for you and you enjoy a communal style of living, in Singapore you will find plenty of cheap places to stay overnight.

ABC Premium Hostel

ABC Premium Hostel has become favored by backpackers and low-budget travelers due to its beneficial location (very near Mustafa centre and Farrer Park MRT station). The beds are clean and comfortable and the basic amenities are provided (shower, toilet, computers, wi-fi, tv and kitchen). For small amount of money you can also have your clothes washed. The hostel also provides nice, simple breakfast. The price range varies from S$23 to S$66 depending on the season and chosen room category.

ABC Premium Hostel, 91A, 93A & 95A Owen Road,

Farrer Park, Singapore 218903, Singapore

Phone: [+65 6298 9390](#)

Hostel Fernloft Chinatown

Hostel Fernloft Chinatown is place that truly represents 'value for money'. Even though it is considered budget accommodation (the night there will cost you from S$19 to S$25) the level of comfort is undoubtedly high. Not only you will receive comfortable and fresh bed in a light and lovely room but you will also be awarded with a superb and warm welcome by the lovely hostess Auntie Aini! Moreover, it is the best choice if you decide to explore Singapore's China Town.

Hostel Fernloft Chinatown, Blk 5 Banda Street #02-92, located on second floor, Singapore 050005 , Singapore

Monni Gallery Hostel

Another option for those traveling on a budget is the Monni Gallery Hostel. The interior and exterior of Monni Hostel is chic and modern, offering very good service for reasonable prices. There are both mixed and female-only dorms that provide air conditioning, shared kitchen, clean shower facilities, library and self-service laundry. Breakfast is included in the price which starts from S$23 per night.

Monni Gallery Hostel, 263 Lavender Street, Little India, 338795 Singapore, Singapore

Phone: +65 6297 6290

E-Mail: enquiry@monigalleryhostel.com

Website: http://www.monigalleryhostel.com/

Mid-range Enclaves

If sharing space with other travelers is not your cup of tea and you are ready to pay a little bit more for your accommodation, there are several recommended mid-range abodes.

Orchard Hotel Singapore

One of such place is the Orchard Hotel Singapore – a comfortable and luxurious hotel located on the resplendent Orchard Road shopping street in the entertainment core of Singapore. All the rooms in Orchard Hotel are well-furnished and neatly designed. The hotel also offers such amenities as an outdoor swimming pool and the Hua Ting Restaurant serving their guests with the best of Cantonese cuisine. The Changi International Airport can be reached in 30 minutes by driving. The price range starts at S$150 per night

Orchard Hotel Singapore, 442 Orchard Road, Orchard, 238879 Singapore, Singapore

Phone: 00 65 6734 7766

E-mail: enquiry.ohs@millenniumhotels.com

Website: http://www.millenniumhotels.com.sg/orchardhotelsingapore/?cid=TAWEBADOHS#_=_

Days Hotel Singapore

Another popular mid-range hotel that can be found in a great location surely is the Days Hotel Singapore at Zhongshan Park. The price range per room per night varies from S$125 to S$230 but all the services and amenities included in this price seem to surpass the value of its modern and spacious rooms, 24 hour fitness center, wonderful restaurant, complementary shuttle to Orchard Road, dry-cleaning and laundry services, among others.

Days Hotel Singapore, 1 Jalan Rajah, Singapore, Singapore 329133

Phone: +65 6808 6838

Website: http://www.dayshotelsingapore.com/

E-mail: reservations@ramada-dayshotelssingapore.com

Parc Sovereign Hotel

If you are seeking a central accommodation that is easily reachable, Parc Sovereign Hotel on Albert Street should be your top-choice. It is a non-smoking hotel that incorporates a variety of quality services such as individually furnished rooms, fitness center, outdoor pool, business center, free parking space and dry-cleaning services. The price of a room starts from S$100 per night.

Parc Sovereign Hotel- Albert St., 175 Albert Street Singapore 189970 Singapore

Phone: 6337 6888

Website: http://www.parcsovereign.com/parc-sovereign

Deluxe Accommodations

Marina Bay Sands Singapore

As much as Singapore is suitable for budget travelers and modest explorers, it also is a superb destination for those who like to travel in luxury. There are numerous 4- and 5-star hotels in Singapore providing an upscale accommodation experience.

Marina Bay Sands has become almost an icon of city with its solid and impressive towers becoming imprescriptible part of the city's panorama. The hotel is comprised of a rooftop infinity pool, casino, 20 restaurants, spa centre, night-club and many other facilities treating each visitor in truly pampered manner. The price range is in accordance with the service, so be ready to pay from S$430 to even S$1200 per night in Marina Bay Sands.

Marina Bay Sands Singapore, 10 Bayfront Avenue, Marina Bay, 018956 Singapore, Singapore

Phone: +65 6688 8888

Website: http://www.marinabaysands.com/index.html

The St Regis Singapore

St Regis hotels are known worldwide and it is a brand that represents high quality standards and elite experiences. St Regis Hotel in Singapore offers an extensive range of deluxe rooms and suites that includes long list of amenities such as 5-star spa centres, fitness centre, butler service, indoor tennis court, meeting organizator and mmore. The hotel is located in the heart of the most prestigeous part of the city thus making it the best choice for those who demand the very best.

The St Regis Singapore, 29 Tanglin Road Singapore 247911

Phone: 656 506 6888

E-mail: stregis.singapore@stregis.com

Website: http://www.stregissingapore.com/

Marina Mandarine Singapore

Situated in the very heart of the city, Marina Mandarine Singapore delivers top-notch experiences and services, treating its guests in the most individual and luxurious manner possible. What you get while staying at this exclusive 5-star hotel is more than just a great room with breathtaking view over the city. On top of that you also are welcomed to use 24-hour fitness center, St Gregory Spa and its 3 restaurants. The visitors have acknowledged the hotel to be a perfect place for both relaxation and entertainment.

Marina Mandarin Singapore, 6 Raffles Boulevard, Marina Square, Marina Bay, 039594 Singapore, Singapore

Phone: (65) 6845 1000

Website: http://www.meritushotels.com/marina-mandarin-singapore/default-en.html

CONCLUSION

Singapore is a place that inspires and provides never-ending creativity for the enthusiastic traveler. Here you will find activities and opportunities that suit every type of traveler – from young backpackers on their way to independent explorations to business travelers seeking prestige and luxury.

Singapore is a one-of-a-kind destination to visit so do not hesitate a single minute to plunge yourself into this ever-bustling and colorful city! Singapore is one of the most thrilling and innovative destinations in the world offering seemingly infinite opportunities for enjoyment.

From a vast range of entertainment activities to numerous remarkable historical, religious and nature sites – all of which greets each traveler with a warm welcome. Hopefully, during this three-day tour you received clear insight into the various sides of Singaporean culture; not only learning something new but also engaging in all the proposed activities with all your heart and soul. Stay curious and keep exploring! Selamat tinggal

MORE FROM THIS AUTHOR

Below you'll find some of our other books that are popular on Amazon and Kindle as well. Alternatively, you can visit our author page on Amazon to see other work done by us.

3 Day Guide to Berlin: A 72-hour definitive guide on what to see, eat and enjoy in Berlin, Germany

3 Day Guide to Vienna: A 72-hour definitive guide on what to see, eat and enjoy in Vienna Austria

3 Day Guide to Santorini: A 72-hour definitive guide on what to see, eat and enjoy in Santorini Greece

3 Day Guide to Provence: A 72-hour definitive guide on what to see, eat and enjoy in Provence, France

3 Day Guide to Istanbul: A 72-hour definitive guide on what to see, eat and enjoy in Istanbul, Turkey

3 Day Guide to Budapest: A 72-hour Definitive Guide on What to See, Eat and Enjoy in Budapest, Hungary

3 Day Guide to Venice: A 72-hour Definitive Guide on What to See, Eat and Enjoy in Venice, Italy

3 Day Guide to Dublin: A 72-hour Definitive Guide on What to See, Eat and Enjoy in Dublin, Ireland

Printed in Great Britain
by Amazon